Dancing Day

A cycle of traditional Christmas Carols

Arranged for S.S.A. voices
and Harp (or Piano)

by John Rutter

Commissioned by the West Midlands Arts Association
and given its first performance in Coventry Cathedral
on 26 January 1974

MUSIC DEPARTMENT

OXFORD
UNIVERSITY PRESS

Contents

Duration 22 minutes

A separate harp part is on sale.

The vocal score is also available on hire.

for Muriel Liddle

DANCING DAY

JOHN RUTTER

Part I
PRELUDE

Printed in Great Britain

OXFORD UNIVERSITY PRESS, MUSIC DEPARTMENT, GREAT CLARENDON STREET, OXFORD OX2 6DP

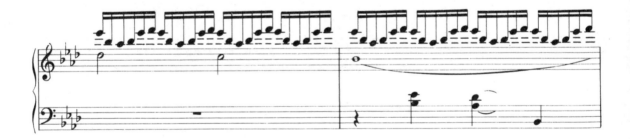

Poco più mosso (♩ = c. 108)

4

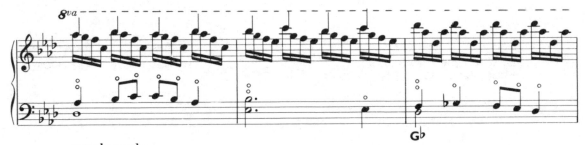

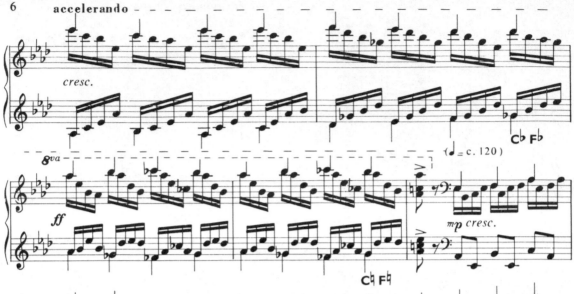

1. ANGELUS AD VIRGINEM

Words and melody
14th century

8

VERSE 2

S.1 — 2. Th'an-gel to the Vir-gin said, En-t'ring in-to____ her bo - wer, For

S.2 — 2. Th'an-gel to the Vir-gin said, En-t'ring in-to her bo - wer, For

A. — 2. Th'an-gel to the Vir-gin said, En-t'ring in-to____ her bo - wer, For

mf Tacet or play colla voce

G♭   G♮

dread of qua-king of this maid, He said 'Hail', with great ho -nou - re. 'Hail!' be thou

dread of qua-king of this maid, He said 'Hail', with great ho -nou - re. 'Hail!' be thou

dread of qua-king of this maid, He said 'Hail', with great ho - nou - re. 'Hail!' be thou

G♭   G♮

-kind. He will make the gate—of hea- ven bright, Med-'cine of all our— sin.'

-kind. He will make the gate—of hea- ven bright, Med-'cine of all our— sin.'

-kind. He will make the gate—of hea- ven bright, Med-'cine of all our— sin.'

G♭   G♮

VERSE 3

mf SOPRANOS

3.'Quo - mo-do con - ci - pe-rem Quae vi - rum non co - gno - vi? Qua - li - ter in-

mf

SOPRANOS
f and ALTOS

-frin - ge-rem Quod fir - ma-men - te vo - vi?' 'Spi - ri - tus

f

G♭

2. A VIRGIN MOST PURE

Words and melody
English traditional

pro - phets do tell, Hath brought forth a ba - by, as it hath be - fel, To

be our Re - deem - er from death, hell, and sin, Which A - dam's trans-

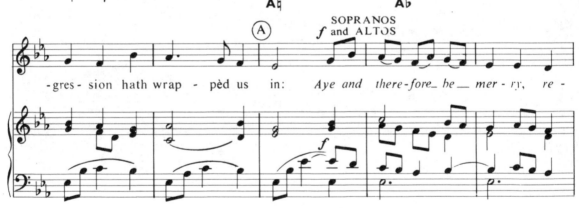

Ⓐ SOPRANOS and ALTOS

-gres - sion hath wrap - pèd us in: Aye and there-fore be merry, re-

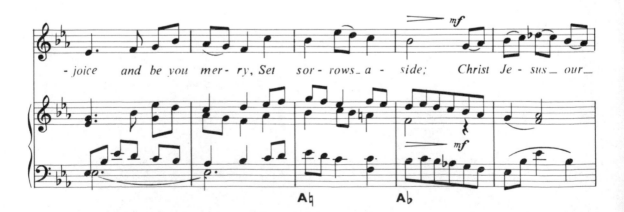

-joice and be you mer - ry, Set sor - rows a - side; Christ Je - sus our

VERSE 2
SOPRANOS
and ALTOS

Sa - viour was born on this tide. 2. At __ Beth-lem __ in __

Jew-ry a ci - ty there was, Where Jo - seph and __ Ma-ry to - ge - ther did

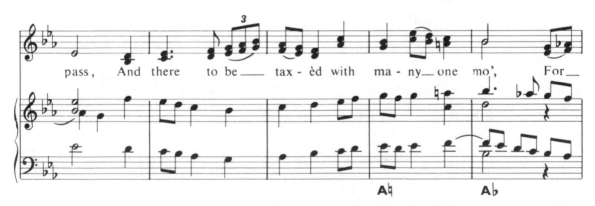

pass, And there to be __ tax - èd with ma - ny __ one mo', For __

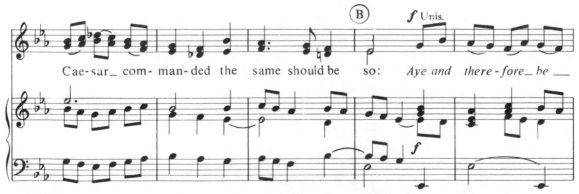

Cae-sar __ com - man-ded the same should be so: *Aye and there-fore __ be* __

14

mer - ry, re - joice and be you mer - ry, Set sor - rows _ a - side; Christ _

Je - sus _ our _ Sa - viour was born on this tide.

VERSE 3

S. 1 3. But _ when they had en - tered the ci - ty so fair, _ A

S. 2 3. But _ when _ they _ had en - tered the ci - ty so fair, A _

A. 3. But when they had en - tered the ci - ty so fair, A _

Tacet or play colla voce

num-ber of peo-ple so migh-ty was there, That Jo-seph and Ma-ry, whose

num-ber of peo-ple so migh-ty was there, That Jo-seph and Ma-ry, whose

num-ber of peo-ple so migh-ty was there, That Jo-seph and Ma-ry, whose

Db   Db

sub-stance was small, Could find in the inn there no lod-ging at

sub-stance was small, Could find in the inn there no lod-ging at

sub-stance was small, Could find in the inn there no lod-ging at

A♮   A♮   Db   Db

SOPRANO or ALTO SOLO

4. Then they were con-strain'd in a sta-ble to lie, Where ox-en and ass-es they used for to tie; Their lod-ging so simple, they held it no scorn, But a-gainst the next morn-ing our Sa-viour was

18

* A cut may be made from here to the asterisk at the bottom of p. 20.

there - fore be _ mer - ry, re - joice and be you mer - ry, Set sor - rows_ a -

Ah

-side; Christ Je - sus_ our_ Sa - viour was born on this tide.

mp

A♭   D♭

* VERSE 6
mp

S.1

SOLO or Ah
TUTTI mf

S.2

6. Then God sent_ an_ an - gel from hea - ven so high, To _ cer - tain_ poor_

A.

mp

Ah   Ah

* Tacet (for rehearsal only)

D♭   D♭

VERSE 7

3. PERSONENT HODIE

Words and melody from
Piae Cantiones (1582)

SOPRANOS and ALTOS

Vivace e ritmico ($\sbond$ = c. 96) *marcato*

1. Per - so - nent ho - di - e Vo - ces pu - e - ru - lae,

Lau - dan - tes ju - cun - de Qui no - bis est na - tus, Sum - mo De - o da - tus,

Et de vir, vir, vir, Et de vir, vir, vir, Et de vir - gi - ne - o

ven - tre pro - cre - a - tus.

SOPRANOS

2. In mun-do na-sci-tur, Pan-nis in - vol-vi-tur, Prae-se - pi po-ni-tur

Verse 2

Sta-bu-lo bru - to - rum, Rec-tor su-per - no - rum. Per-di -dit - dit, - dit,

D♭

Ⓑ Per-di-dit, -dit, -dit, Per-di-dit spo-li - a prin-ceps in-fer - no - rum.

D♮

S. 1
   2

3. Ma - gi tres ve - ne - runt, Par - vu - lum

A.

3. Ma - gi tres ve - ne - runt, Par - vu - lum

Verse 3

Tacet - *for rehearsal only*

28

SOPRANOS and ALTOS

4. Om-nes cle - ri-cu-li, Pa-ri-ter

(A♮)

A♭

E♭

unis.

pu-e ri, Can-tent ut an-ge-li: Ad-ve-ni-sti mun - do,

E♭

A♮

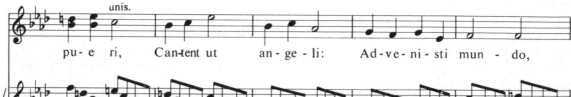

D cresc.

Lau-des ti-bi fun - do. I - de-o, - o, - o, I - de-o,

A♭

allargando

- o, - o, I - de-o glo-ri-a in ex-cel-sis De - o.

A♭

E♭

Part II
INTERLUDE

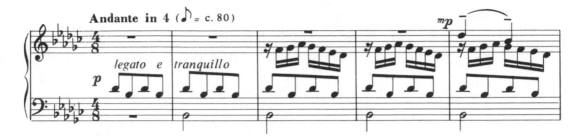

rit. molto - - - - - a tempo

tranquillo, non marcato

4. THERE IS NO ROSE

Voice parts and words
15th century *

S. 1/2

Flowingly (♩ = c. 120)

mp legato

There is no (no) rose of ___ such ___ vir - tue

A.

mp legato

Flowingly (♩ = c. 120)

ppp   mf

* From the edition by John Stevens by permission of Stainer & Bell Ltd.

VERSES 1 and 2

S.

mf dolce

Soli 1. There is ____ no rose of such ____ vir - tue As ____
All 2. For in ____ this rose con - tain - èd ____ was Hea -

A.

mf dolce

is ____ the rose that bare Je - su. Al - le -
-ven and earth in ____ lit - tle space. Res ____ mi -

D. S. for
Verse 2

- lu - - - - - ia. ____
- ran - - - - - da. ____

As is the rose that bare Je - su.

mp *p*

Ⓐ (after V. 2)

There is no rose of ___ such ___ vir - tue   As

is the rose ___ that ___ bare ___ Je - su. ___

attacca

C♮, A♮

5. COVENTRY CAROL

Words from the Pageant of the
Shearmen and Tailors, 15th century

Voice parts slightly adapted
from a Ms. of 1591

Andante con moto (♩ = c. 96)

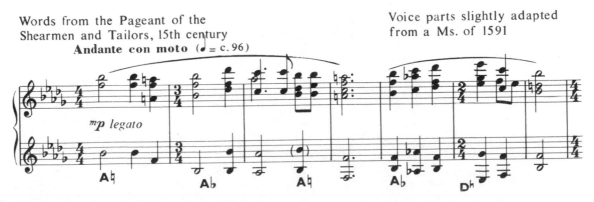

mp legato

A♮   A♭   A♮   A♭   D♭

Lul - ly, lul - la, thou lit - tle ti - ny child, By by, lul - ly, lul - lay, thou lit - tle ti - ny child, By by, lul - ly, lul - lay.

Db, A♮   A♭   A♮   A♭   D♮

C♯   C♮ D♭   A♮   D♮

VERSE 1

1. O sis - ters too, How may we _ do For to pre - serve this _ day This

D♭   A♭   A♮   A♭   D♮ C♯

For whom we do sing,

poor young-ling For whom we do sing, By by, lul - ly lul - lay?

For whom we do sing,

C♮,D♭ A♮ D♮ A♭

VERSE 2

f marcato

S.
A.

2. He - rod the king, In his ra - ging, Char - ged he

simile

D♭,G♮

hath this day His men of might, In his own

sim.

E♮,A♮

sight, All young chil - dren to slay.

VERSE 3

3. That woe is me, Poor child for_ thee! And ev - er

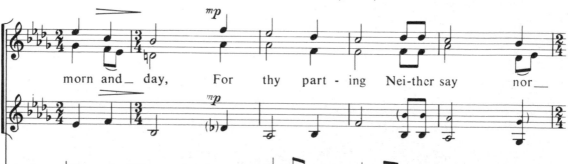

morn and_ day, For thy part - ing Nei-ther say nor_

sing By by, lul - ly lul - lay! Lul - ly, lul -

- la, thou lit - tle ti-ny child, By by, lul - ly, lul -

- lay, thou lit - tle ti-ny child, By by, lul - ly, lul - lay.

6. TOMORROW SHALL BE MY DANCING DAY

Words and melody
English traditional

39

-mor-row shall be _ my danc-ing day: I would my true_love did _ so

chance To_ see the le-gend of_ my play, To call my true_love

to _ my dance: Sing O my_ love, O _ my love, my

love. my love; This have I done_for my_ true love.

VERSE 2

VERSE 3

3. In a man - ger laid _ and wrapp'd I

was, So ve - ry poor, _ this was _ my chance, Be - twixt an

ox and a sil - ly poor ass, To call my true _ love to _ my dance: Sing

44

Ⓓ

ALL VOICES

To-mor-row shall be_ my danc-ing day: I would_my true_love did_ so chance To_

see the le - gend of_ my play, To call my true_ love

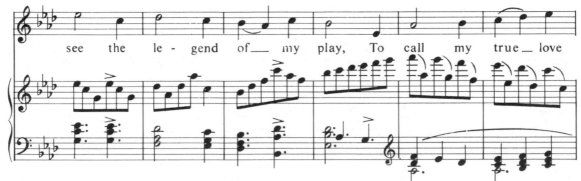

Ⓔ

S. 1

to_ my dance: Sing O my_ love, O __ my

S. 2
A.

to_ my dance: Sing O my_ love, O __ my love, my

SOPRANOS
1 and 2

love, my love; This have I done for my true love, this

ALTOS

love, my love; This have I done for my true love, this

Largamente _ _ _ _ _ _ _ _ _ _ _ _ _ _ _ a tempo (non dim.)

have I done _ _ for my _ true love.

(non dim.)

have I done _ _ for my _ true love.

Largamente _ _ _ _ _ _ _ _ a tempo

Gb   Cb   Fb   F♮, C♮

(senza rall.)

Ab major 8va
gliss.

Gb   Cb, Fb   F♮, C♮ G♮

Reproduced and printed by
Halstan & Co. Ltd., Amersham, Bucks., England